I0617042

First paperback edition April 2025

Cover Art by Sarah Chayer

Illustrations by Sarah Chayer

ISBN 979-8-9886525-5-7 (paperback)

ISBN 979-8-9886525-6-4 (ebook)

www.sarahchayer.com

Moonlit Valley

By Sarah Chayer

Dedicated to Gigi, my sister and my hero, who continues to inspire me every day.

Table of Contents

Foreword

In 2021, I started my journey to improve my mental health and self-esteem. I clawed my way out of a terrible place and made it down the metaphorical mountain to a safe valley where I could work on my recovery. But the aforementioned valley was just a rest stop, and I knew I would have another mountain to climb to get to where I wanted to be, and that scared me. After so much anguish to get to a point of safety, I was terrified to step out of that comfort zone. Fortunately, I have a great support system of family and friends, so in 2024, I pushed onward and moved to England to marry my best friend and soulmate.

Healing is not linear. Some days I feel like I've conquered all my past traumas. Some days I wake up feeling like I'm back at square one and can't get out of bed. It's an on-going battle up this mountain and out of my cozy valley, but I'm not making the climb alone.

Since the release of *Moon Rise* in 2023, I have continued to grow. I've continued to use art and poetry as therapeutic coping mechanisms. So, just as I did then, I've collected my favorites to express my continued journey. Perhaps some of it might resonate with and inspire readers.

Ink

Touch the pen to paper
Rest on college rule
But it does not move
Tip to the line
An ocean, a vast nothing
But the growing black
Spidering
Enveloping the page ever slowly
It longs to glide
To drag pleasingly across the white
Instead, it stays
It soaks, draining the ink
The life
Drop by drop
Drip by drip
Starting line hazy
The fog swarms
An entangled web
A tug of war
Knot pulled tighter and tighter
Rooting the point in place
The stain expands
Consuming the page
Extending outward, ominous
Then ends
The pen is empty

Time Traveling

I am a time traveler

Just a blink ago I was a child
A scrawny girl
Sweets and honey-dunked nuggets
Missing teeth
Grass-stained holes in denim knees
Racing to swings
Rolling down hills

Not a moment later
I'm taller
By stature alone
Feel only smaller inside
Shoulders slump
Head bows
Concealed behind my façade
I paint my face
Mismatching colors and dark, rigid lines
Pinching cellulite in the bathroom mirror
Mascara tears behind shut doors

In an instant
I've walked my second stage
Rotated my second tassel
Tossed my second cap
Yet my head hangs lower still

I've grown
In more ways than one
But perhaps regressed a great deal, too
Searching for a romance novel in reality
Though not a love to find
At the bottom of a bottle
Swigging sadness

Another leap forward
Thirty
Knees hurt
Back hurts
There is a world beyond these walls
Beyond blankets and pillows
Closed bedroom shades
A desire to venture
Yet a gravity pulls me back
I stumble along

The magic only works one way
I only launch forward in time
Though I long to return to
That child with grass-stained knees
Or that scrawny teen wearing too much makeup
There is no spell
No incantation
To move backwards

Cherry Blossoms

Tiny white blossoms bloom
Giving way to luscious fruit
Glowing red beads against the summer green
Thousands travel from miles around
To pick the precious berries

Pluck.

Pluck.

Pluck.

One by one
Greedily severed
Desolate greens remain
Eventually the leaves wilt
And they, too, fall away
Until there is nothing left

Brown, bare branches
Naked
Alone
At least 'til spring rolls in again
And so, the cycle goes.

Dungeons of my Mind

It's scary the places your mind can go
The depths to which your thoughts can sink
When at last, you've found the bottom rung
Now you can rest, or so you think

Each and every rickety stairstep
Gives way in your attempt to climb
Strive as you may to seek the surface
Fall through a new basement every time

down

down

down

every time

Imagine a lifeline, a rope out of this pit
Intentional ignorance to this prison below
These dungeons are scary places
How far forgotten can my lonesome thoughts go?

Foggy Moon

Much like the moon tonight
is shrouded in fog
I find my mind a haze

The Happy Parts

Why do I struggle to write about the light?
About the happy parts, the sunshine and smiles
Why do my eyes fall only on the pain I fight?
I see only the darkness, the storms and their trials

Perhaps this thorny nest is what I was born into
The pricks and scratches at a soul begotten
Far are the soft comforts I never knew
Unfamiliar with silk or down or cotton

Reflecting, my life feels a lament
Though I acknowledge more beyond this gloom
Perhaps I believe I deserve punishment
Maybe I'm destined for this self-made tomb

Bleeding Branches

Green dissolves to yellows and reds
Witness the branches bleed
Orange in the air and ground
Leaves and gourds
Like warm, cinnamon-scented snow
Fluttering through the sky
If only I could trap this smell, this day, in a jar
Open for a refreshing essence of spiced autumn breeze
On my worst days
When I need it most

Ribboned

My chest, my air, constricted and ribboned
Dark water surrounds, submerged in bone
But in this catacomb suffers more than one
Ghosts arise, otherworldly allies to lift and lean on

Ma'am

"Ma'am"
Always hated that term

It doesn't ring
As an endearment
Of respect

Regardless
Of your
Intent

I am not old
I am not outdated
I am not inferior

I have a name
Use it

If you don't know it
Ask

My name
Is not
"Ma'am"

Descend

Hold tight to that railing
As you cautiously descend
No telling what dangers await

One misplaced step
One crooked board
Could be your downfall

Thus, I insist again
Hold tight to that railing
As you cautiously descend

The Fortress

Castle walls stand tall around me
While the snowstorm rages on
Shards of ice ripping through me
Freezing gusts blister flesh with each blast

I built this fortress
Erected this stronghold myself
A lonely, icy husk
Trapping this blizzard that I keep whirling
Inside
With me

This barrier I constructed
Surrounding myself
Is designed to withstand the storm
Not to shelter me
But to keep everyone else out
Protected
And safe from the tempest

Day in and day out
The snowflakes fly about
Within these walls
To keep those I love a secure distance

I deserve this
The pain and the loneliness
But everyone should be kept away
Safe
The storm claws at the stone
Desperate to escape
But I must keep it here
Locked in here

This punishment I've cast upon myself
This life sentence
A suiting sanction
For an empty coward

My Children

My little Prince
The Jester
The crier
High-pitched whimper
After whimper
Yet childishly playful
Fetch and return
Baby brother
Ever stupidly fearless
Brave in brother's shadow
Glistening amber eyes
Reflecting every hue of love

My Princess
The Duchess
Wake me at the crack of dawn
Then return to sleep alone
She calls the shots
She sets the timetables
The fastest eater
Greedily
Gobbling up brother's food
With the sharpest teeth
The kick and whine
Demanding attention

My King
My whole heart
Love at first bite
Could never be apart
Fluff and cuddle
Emotional support
Resting on my chest
Washing away the tears
A passive leader
Seen but rarely heard
Forever inviting
Happy to meet

You tried to come that day
You begged
You fought to sneak past
Forced to push you back inside
leaving a part of me
there
with you

Someday
I will have kids
A couple of little tots
They'll have ten toes
Ten tiny fingers
Full heads of hair
My smile and
Their father's eyes

They will have a home
Filled with toys
Filled with music
Filled with love

My children will have all that we can give
But they will never have
Been given the chance
To meet you

My little Prince
My Princess
And my King

Bare Below

Bare branches below the canopy
No sunlight piercing through the tree
Pine needles litter the ground
Everything a sickly shade of brown
While above, summer greens, carefree

Haze And Humidity

Darken skies cast Earth in shadow
Heavenly haze, hellish humidity
'Round me witness abyss grow
Whirling gloom cloud lucidity

Heavenly haze, hellish humidity
Uncover, between, a mediate state
Whirling gloom cloud lucidity
Converge courage to infiltrate

Uncover, between, a mediate state
Somber space of no direction
Converge courage to infiltrate
All-consuming dissociation

Somber space of no direction
'Round me witness abyss grow
All-consuming dissociation
Darken skies cast Earth in shadow

A World Left Behind

My life has no meaning
My trial is complete
My work concluded
The friends I made along my journey
No longer need me
The kingdom saved
The enemy defeated
Caverns and forests
Skies and springs
All that I once explored
Day
After week
After month
Realms that never really existed
But were so very real to me
I've left that world behind
Now I live my own epilogue
With empty hours crushing me
I sit
I can only stare
Blankly
There is no purpose for me now
Until the hero is called upon again

A Party I Wasn't Invited to and Didn't Want to go to Anyway

I hear the beating
The bass and drums
Far away
Thundering approach yet distancing
It's a faded buzz
A growling mosquito
Clawing
Quiet but deep
Scratching at my ear
To ensure it isn't ignored
Isn't forgotten
Clap hands tight against my head
Squeeze shut my eyes
Draw a silent scene
Scout my mind for stillness
But always interrupted
By the persistent pounding
Bum bum bum
A little burn in the duct
A spreading sting
Tight throat
It goes dry and rough
Fidgeting fingers
Twisting rings
Round and round

Cross and uncross legs
Shadows fall upon my face
Slink lower
Cower behind the screen
Thud thud thud
It never ends
How I wish it would end
Just waiting
Mind the minutes
Ticking by
Slower and slower
Counting seconds
Tug my hair and pinch lips
The most disingenuous smile
A "hello" can barely escape me
Dun dun dun
Itching every joint in my being
Pulling me to the back
Behind the walls
Deprived of prying eyes
Gritting teeth
Another minute gone
Finally, a pause
A moment's peace
Is this it?
...
Nope
The bass resumes
Once again

Forest Battlefield

Leaves of every shape
    Some like blades
        Some like shields
            Some like arrows

The forest is a silent battlefield
    Ready in defense
        Of a war we don't yet know

Unhappy Pill

Little pill
Little, round pill
Little, round, white pill

Down you go
Down my throat
Little happy pill

Assume a smile
Abide my trial
Perfect the masking skill

But shields wear thin
Boost serotonin
Request a refill

I shrink, withdrawn
The world spins on
But I'm stranded still

Near comatose
You up my dose
Still tumbling downhill

Shattered with grief
Desperate relief
Refuse to lose my will

Little pill
Little, round pill
Little, round, white pill

Can I repair
Fragile welfare
Little unhappy pill

Haunted

A darkness, a silhouette
Harrowing, haunting, imminent threat
In which the moonlight cannot follow
Looming figure, eye sockets hollow
It approaches, creeping close
Extended arm, ominous and morose
Rooted in place, I'm frozen put
Skeletal fingers, black like soot
Coiling round my neck, stealing breath
Its malicious, melting grin of death
Whirling black mist, rising slow
Seeping from this grim shadow
Engulf the world to my eye alone
Forsaken, an icy heart of stone
Dooming my soul, my life to decay
Sense all light dissolve away
It finally frees me from its grasp
Inhale the darkness when I gasp
Sick and spinning from the attack
Choking while the shape slinks back
A vile smile where its mouth would be
It disposed its desolation onto me
Already I feel the emptiness grow
As I, too, become a shadow

What Good In Me?

It's funny, what my eyes can't see
Sense nothing but dark and ruin
Though you see only good in me

Wither, withdraw, shield and wary
Fragmented, fragile, flawed shut-in
It's funny, what my eyes can't see

Stain of a smile devoid of beauty
Scarred flesh and blemished skin
Though you see only good in me

Perceive, burdened with empathy
Wrinkle, dark circle, evince stress within
It's funny, what my eyes can't see

Bury myself in pillows and pity
Wallow in shallow water, bow my violin
Though you see only good in me

Funhouse mirror body, misshapen, ugly
Rolls and folds, far the figure once I'd been
It's funny, what my eyes can't see
Though you see only good in me

Dissociation

She is a character
Written by someone else

She may look like me
But I don't know who she is

She was created for better things

She was authored for a life of meaning
She was perfectly scripted
To fall into place
Illustrating a complete picture

She may wear my face
But I don't know who she is

Not Okay

I'm not okay today
Feel my mind decay
Tortured thought ballet
Under darkness weigh
A bluish, blackish gray
Stranded here, I stay
Caught in a thorn bouquet
Can't free myself away
Consumed, I only lay
Cry for light and pray
Promise to obey
And every cent I'd pay
If only for a way
To keep the dark at bay
Though sound it cliché
Remind myself to say
I'm not okay today
But know that it's okay
Tomorrow's a new day

Rest

Rest my mind through night to reset, *set*
An alarm to aid me to rise, e*yes*
Swollen and puffy at light of day, *a*
New opportunity to learn and adjust, *just*
One more day to grow stronger still, *til*
My next sleep after, this day I will crest

Morning Loon

Tranquility

Not a ripple on the bay

Nor a morning breeze to disrupt the crystal shores

Save a lone loon

A silhouette lost in pastels

Floating amongst the gold-lined clouds

With a shake of his feathered head

The bird dives beneath the mirror

And disappears into the sky

Walk

In a steel bird amongst the blue
Far from life's crowd
The world often out of view
Beneath waves of cloud

Or racing onward in a train
Down track following routine
Disconnect from time's mundane
The scene outside, a tv screen

Silence thoughts, shut down my mind
Locked on the steering wheel
Moments lost, I can't rewind
The blur outside, surreal

Now on pedals, slow my tempo
Falsely feel autonomy
Opportunity to stop or slow
Yet speed will still rob me

But walking on my own two feet
The only chance to take control
Embrace each second, sour or sweet
Choose to sit, sprint, or stroll

Toes in green, floral scents
Raindrops and fluttering snow
I claim all my moments
Won't lose them out the window

Swing

Can't get a hit if I don't swing
Breathe in deep before I take wing
Grateful for each chance, lose or win
Seize life's joy, soak it all in

Waiting For Me

I pack up all
I can fit

In a suitcase
Two or three

Though nervous
I admit

New adventures
Wait for me

Zip shut my
Many bags

For flight over
Land and sea

Equipped with
Luggage tags

New journeys
Wait for me

Crowd in a
Piled airplane

Alone in my
Mind only

When I land
I will gain

A new life
Waiting for me

About the Author

Sarah Chayer published her first novel, *Incandescent: Magic Unknown*, in 2022 and a book of poetry, *Moon Rise,* in 2023. Work on the *Incandescent* series is ongoing, as well as a second, separate series, but Sarah wanted to publish a continuation of her personal mental health journey, following that of her previous book of poetry, in hopes that the artistic depiction of her battle with depression, anxiety, and low self-esteem might help or inspire others facing their own struggles.

Sarah graduated cum laude with a Bachelor of Arts Degree for Communication emphasis in Journalism from the University of Wisconsin - Green Bay and has won awards for her work in fiction, poetry, and English. She moved to England in 2024 and is happily married to her best friend and biggest supporter.

www.ingramcontent.com/pod-product-compliance
Lightning Source LLC
Chambersburg PA
CBHW051648120626
46551CB00015B/2267